AFTERIMAGES

AFTERIMAGES

POEMS BY

CATHRYN HANKLA

LOUISIANA STATE UNIVERSITY PRESS

BATON ROUGE AND LONDON

1991

Designer: Laura Roubique Gleason
Typeface: Granjon
Typesetter: Graphic Composition, Inc.
Printer and binder: Thomson-Shore, Inc.

Library of Congress Cataloging-in-Publication Data

Hankla, Cathryn, 1958–
    Afterimages : poems / by Cathryn Hankla.
      p. cm.
    ISBN 0-8071-1684-X (cloth).—ISBN 0-8071-1685-8 (paper)
    I. Title: After images.
  PS3558.A4689A69   1991
  811'.54—dc20   90-27598
                                                                                      CIP

The author offers grateful acknowledgment to the editors of the following periodicals, in which poems in this volume first appeared: *Artemis,* "Ashes, Ashes," "Island, Perhaps"; *College English,* "A Way to Dance," "Morning Half-Light," "For My Cousins"; *Denver Quarterly,* "Puritan"; *Images,* "Positive," "Magnification/Abstraction"; *Mississippi Valley Review,* "Little Deaths"; *Missouri Review,* "Flight Luck," "Lighting the Dark Side of the Moon"; *New Virginia Review,* "Double Drowning," "Night Trip," "The Tautology of Goodbye," "Five Years from the Last Five Minutes of Your Life," "In Focus," "Prayer Upon Parting"; *Woman Poet: The South,* "Tree in the Rock," "*A Lady Writing a Letter* by Vermeer," "*Lady Reading a Letter at the Open Window* by Vermeer"; *Yarrow,* "Dear Friends," "Feeding the Frozen Animals." "Island, Perhaps" also appeared in the *Anthology of Magazine Verse & Yearbook of American Poetry, 1986–88,* ed. Alan Pater (New York, 1988).

The author would like to thank Randolph-Macon Woman's College for a residency during which several of these poems were written or begun; Carole Oles, Lynne Spies, and Dara Wier for advice on arrangement and individual poems; and Sandra O'Connell of Washington and Lee University for secretarial finesse.

The paper in this book meets the guidelines for permanence and durability of the Committee on Production Guidelines for Book Longevity of the Council on Library Resources.⊗

in memory

CONTENTS

AFTERIMAGES

DOUBLE DROWNING

I can recall the movie
in Driver's Ed
of mannequin couples throwing their love
through windshields
because of what they were not wearing.

And in this vein, I remember
my Sr. Life Saving course that cold winter,
the license uncrimped in my wallet,
when I went to the Y after supper
to swim required distances.
I'd walk out into snowy nights,
my hair lightly frozen by the time I drove home,
alone with an unexpected memory
stalking back
                of the horse who ripped a hole
bigger than three fists in his breast
and stood with a twitch of leather
gripping his muzzle
so he might forget the larger pain
while the vet cleaned his wound with a garden hose,
sending streams of startling color
into parched ground at my shoes. I could not look
away, I could not watch, I could not
say what I had come for, I could not forget.
Driving home I saw the dark
circles flower into me
and stopped the car in time
to topple. The steering wheel stopped me.
I awakened, a dream later, weak, trembly,
and drifted toward home, through the door,
to hear my mother question,
"Did you get the job?"
"I didn't ask," I said

and saw her catch my expression as she turned
and saw her rush in slow motion, as if through water,
forever holding out her arms
for fear of my falling.

                    The final night
our teacher dressed in army boots, fatigues, and chains
and threw himself into the deepest part of the olympic pool.
We were to save him any way we could, then pull
his weight one length before lifting his lungs to air.
It was worse than the warm-up test
when we jumped in carrying a mask
and snorkel, cleared the mask underwater, blew the last
of our breath out the snorkel
and continued to swim without our heads' surfacing.
It was worse than the cinder block.
But I forget exactly how that worked.

He flailed, looking more like he wanted to kill
than to sink. He pushed the buoyant objects
from him, lunged expertly toward my neck, interlocking
his fists. We went down six feet
while I only kept my head by thinking
what might happen if he ever let a student die like this.
I pushed his hips up, turned him, locked my arms, my fingers
barely meeting around the beef of his chest, rose
briefly, and rode him as if he were an octopus.
Spinning over and over, we inched toward the shallows.
Biting for air, holding on, held fast, pressing
an elbow into his heart, I kicked for all my life.

A vivid picture of double drowning lingers
in my mind
                the entwined couple in Russell's "Women in Love"
                hug against the drained pond's silt
                like fossils

of what might happen if one were to approach
a victim
without proper precaution.

       Better to let one drown than to
have entered the water
and bobbled down
down to the waiting weeds of some green lake
or river bottom
or other
down below day-
light, where no wind can stir the mirror
into shared circles of this perfect life.

NIGHT TRIP

Father comes for you, scoops you up
from dreams into his crazy arms, tucks
you into the large backseat
of his Buick Skylark. Too sleepy
to ask a simple *Why?* or *Where?*
too small to question, you must
pull knees to meet your chest,
and travel as he drives you,
home, but first around fast twists
of unlimited access, past objects
left to imagination, in the dead
night of the fields and farther out
beyond the crisp white fences,
as you attempt sleep, spinning over
animals that happen under
his wheels; and you
cannot know his whole face,
this man, tattooed with speed and dark.

This is why, for the rest of your life,
when someone asks you to come
you will, yet resist against reason,
against hope, while you wait
for betrayal, invite it by mistrust,
wait for a car to lurch at ravines.

MY AUNTS SHOW ME THEIR HAIR

On a night with no moon
they trek to the attic
above their room
and bring two thin, blue boxes
down for me to view—
the paper coverings torn, bruised
by dark. I open a box
after its twin: braids
from nineteen-twenty, two coils
of auburn flappers shed.
Now the waves on their heads,
magically white, glow silver-blue
when caught by light. They laugh
because I'm scared to lift
the twisted locks off tissue beds.
My aunts pick up their caches,
as fragile as rotten string,
and bobby pin those tails
at the nape of my neck. *Here's
Grandmother's hand-mirror,* they chant.
I take the oval, spin
before the cheval glass
and hold just so, once
I've whirled like a world,
to balance twin images,
to attend a matched reflection
of old hair against my own.
My aunts sit down to pincurls,
combs, their nightly ritual.
I steady grandmother's mirror,
with one hand pull the pins,
and for a second
the braids, against my skin,
hesitate to fall.

*for Marjorie Sarah Burnette, and in memory of
Margaret Ella Burnette, 1907–1988*

ASHES, ASHES

The boy back-diving
into death, slowly circling
head to tail.

In his last months
he resembled a flailing
fish held up into the air
by a hook.

Inevitable, they said.
In time his heart would punch
a hole just large enough
for his life to fall through.

We worried why
he had to come to school.

The very sick wish to be
like everyone else,
my mother said. *Why?*
Especially those dying.
They wish to hate school like you,
but for them it doesn't work—

whenever they wake,
hear the chains of the bus tires
singing over snow,
they are happy.
They can't wait to go.

LITTLE DEATHS

The mockingbird returned
as she was meant to; I do not know
the meaning of inevitability, but she—
who had flown free to nest in fronds
and teach her brood—to fly
into our chimney a second time,
would choose a morning no one was home
nor would return two weeks.
I know how traitors must feel,
if anyone has died on behalf
of lies they told. If we had not left
the retreat of mountains for the moving edges
of sea, the mockingbird might be
migrating the south flyway. The signs
she left: splatters of soot pushed through
the slatted fireguard onto the brick hearth,
little tracks etching the baked ash bed.
Exhausted, her head lay close to glass
in her simoom so that she saw at last
the room was clear. When her body filled
a brass shovel, it had no weight.
When fitted into a paper sack,
it took the character of air; its lack
of resistance lent false buoyancy to lift.
I rested the sack on shells
collected after a hurricane threat.
For a week or more, we shied from burial.

■

The faithful Shadow, and Jane
our tortoise-shell cat: these winter deaths
and other, summer ones: a young opossum
at the crossing, a snow white rabbit,
a box turtle cracked by a truck;
the mockingbird, a pair of tropical
fish, a left-handed whelk. A boy
down the street met death;

now his dog is a wanderer who barks
when convertibles swerve the curve.
A blue jay, injured irreparably,
died in the greenhouse undisturbed by toms.

Today in late September, early fall,
you and I walk our circuit, see a snake
studded by a tire; we remember
the copperhead we should have killed
as it sunned, camouflaged on the drive.
At supper you forget, recalling Oliver,
a long-kept pet; from habit you set
your plate down for his lick; you stop,
a maple syrup ring unfinished.
I feel us counting up the little deaths
between us
as I catch and hold your eyes.
After I am sleeping at your side, you sleep
better for the cat curled near your thigh—

until a dream turns back into the night,
and we hear an animal siren quiver round the hill.
In the morning we search the wind, we listen, yes,
it swills the air; we shiver when this wail pinches
shut, a wound held; sensing no sign
of what it is, we stumble windward, tense;
we hum some tune not strummed before,
we run, return home,
where the door hangs open on its hinge.

THE FIRST DAY
OF CHRISTMAS

The couple watched TV
after supper

waiting for the bullet
to enter the husband

to pierce the heart
of his knee

so now he cannot walk
or work and there is no

grease to boil
the string beans.

The window did not break.

■

You ask me of relevance
in a world

where an eleven-year-old
girl skipping

home with a loaf
of day-old bread can be

raped beneath a bridge at noon
tied with her clothes

and left to die a day before
Thanksgiving.

■

I used to have an answer
now I have another:

No one knows
who fired the shot.

The rapist had just
been let go by his boss.

Either you're a friend
or you aren't:

I cannot promise
never to do wrong.

DEAR FRIENDS

There is no such thing as perfect communication
as our train whistles north through fields
of broken pines that my eyes climb
branch after broken branch to their needled
widow's walks. I look out over this landscape,

panning through the movie it becomes,
and my mind wanders until I see, more
clearly than ever before, your
faces. Each window frames a changing composition,
sometimes my own face, that registers only as afterimage.

The conductor's voice sweeps the car,
our cawing whistle stops as he tells us the time
has leapt ahead to Eastern Standard.
It's no surprise, for I have left
behind so many times, that only time, I fear,

can tell how long it will take
to come here again. Up ahead
the engine rounds a bend, almost knotting our train
into a circle, unfurling as we keep pace
on the track. If this motion should stop, my heart

would jump back, my head
balk, impatient to see the problem solved,
to be under way without the lingering whiplash
of memory. But it's not to be
so simple, friends.

We pass another stretch of calf-speckled green,
their white faces flash, while the black boy sleeps on
his mother's breast, and the man who's lost his children
talks, and the girls who want
another Lucky step

into the aisle streaming cologne
that wakes some speculation.
I try not to stare too long at anyone
but it's harder to stay aloof
than to touch

each seatback for balance as I rock along
this car into another and still others, finally
popping out onto the swaying platform
to look back
into the funnel of swirling color

where you wave, surely
moving your free hands back and forth in the air.
I can remember the ex-marine's story:
My boy's only twenty
but he looks like thirty. His mother stole

him and his brother from me years ago.
I got this photograph, no letter. You want to see
my tattoos? I looked at my boy's face and never felt
so sorry in my life. Look here, at this heart,
inside it says, "glory."

MORNING HALF-LIGHT

Lover, who has
held my grief when
family left
this world and me,

it is morning,
and I see you,
blurry, but in
motion, holding

eggs. The kitchen
scramble—skillet,
butter, toast, and
radio news—

reveals that you
put on a show,
eating only,
I think, to make

me feel better
for surviving.
You pass through this
morning half-light

like air itself,
while I mutter,
as through needles'
eyes the camels

squeeze. Easier
to ponder than
to do. I know,
by instinct's far

backwaters, you
must be real, or
the only true
gravity here,

because it was
you who said, it
was you who said,
Let me make love

to you, because
you hold inside
memories, lost
faces of kin.

THE ANGEL ON THE CEILING

After sex
you scratched a message across my shoulder
blades. (I thought back to that day
you drew the hexagram *Fu* up my spine—
five broken horizons
above a fine yang line:

I had to find its name, what it meant
in *The Book of Change,* before I could
answer you with truth, with what
you already knew—
yes, at the winter solstice
I would return to you.)

My first deciphering failed utterly.
I turned and faced up. A shadow
the clock made, a shot
of light through the lampshade.
I said *bat,* because I saw
a fixed, black bird.

You wrote the word,
index in air, and I thought
the shadow of wings edged
in a show of hovering:
                          your message
went unread upon the dark.

Angel, you said and pointed up.
I felt the word, distinct
on my skin, a repetition
mysteriously meant. By your gesture,
I saw on the ceiling a rare vision:
an angel, dark and still.

Until we turned the lamp
on, wings hovered there
and would return, invisibly with the light
above: the tangible unseen
of the shadow seen. Or an act of love,
turning in the dark to gesture all the time

toward what it is not, touching
to sense what cannot be touched.

TWO HANDS UNDER PRESSURE

Ringed and watched, scarred, mottled, lost
hand, you do nothing without my thinking:
lift the teacup, trace my mood. I blink; you
follow, blue, like the hound you have gone
to rub, far back in memory.

Hand, how much you sense that's mine in touching
other things. When you grow cool I know I am
alone. On a hillside you palm air for clues;
at the crosswalk pat, pat your pocket lining,
thumb lint, and stretch open
to wave the space between friends.

■

Round pads, pawlike, unlike zebra's
hooves or alphabet curves:
to construct this language
one hand must lie at rest.

Variegated, plump on the desk,
my busy hand, abstract as a mouse in a trap
of words, taps, taps out the signs
by which it is known: *bleak boredom* or *salute*.
I read: *a carriage trail, damp ruts in woods,*
as clearly as your hand raised to leave.

TREE IN THE ROCK

A pin point man playing a hand line
like a marionette, little hooks for arms, legs.
A flounder underneath the bridge
seeing rivulets of sun. A woman
seeing from afar, through a crack,
hairline of breath in the isinglass: a man,
motionless, except his fingering of the string,
music above the waving fish.

A man smiling in a pin-striped, railroad
cap; this man holding out a sack
crimped at the top. A girl lifting it
out of his hands like a laugh. His hands
make a church, then a whistle
that will take years for her to follow.
When she opens the sack, inside
nestle hundreds of brown, shiny
nuts. The man slits one with his pocketknife,
thumbs back the shell like polished paper;
he points the blade to the green porcupine
beneath the tree. She throws the fruit,
iced green, to air and tongues the chestnut
back, a lump in her throat
when it rains and will not stop,
and mist reminds her when she stoops
to take the lost bag of chestnuts,
a sudden autumn gift. Her breath whistles
back into her throat
where the face of the man is
smiling beyond death, pushing this wad of chestnuts
forward to her fingertips
like a live bouquet of tulips out of earth.

A photograph: tree in the rock.
Tree like a spine sprouting
from granite; roots that sift the grainy
soil into a dream of permanence. It's always

a dream, this rising, tree in the rock, out of nothing
in defiance of law, chaos, codes
of sea, the tree grows straight
to the stars. See its bark layered in the hide
of years rings cannot reckon.
Why do you look for the living among the dead?
The life of rocks   a sign in trees
in defiance of signs   a sign in the rocks
in defiance of earth   a river of rocks
in defiance of rivers, of earths, lifting toward air
out of nothing   into the cleanliness   of something
into the sun
tree in the rock.
Spine of the earth, let me count the twigs that compass
your strength greater than any winged thing,
above even angels printed on snow, living through rock
and making it so
move.
Rose tree, its bloom frozen of a frost:
a rose, a tree, from the death of rock.
Judge not   judge not   judge not.
A tree rose from the death of a rock, tree
in the rock, a living tree
in the rock.

in memory of Kirt Dickerson, 1893–1980

MAGNIFICATION/ABSTRACTION

A spot of snow
ablaze beneath
sunlight shines briefly
brighter than snow could ever be,
before extinction
turns its flare, its whiter than white,
into an expression of blue,
blue water reflecting clouds.

■

Every child has held
the sun inside herself
by holding still a magnifying glass
to focus light
until a leaf ignites.

Sunlight that used to be
everywhere at once, the fact,
say, of blue sky,
reveals itself as an object,
a spot in time, like the spot
of fire seeming to leap
from inside the leaf.

■

If language finds this difficult
then I must know the secret, why
the word without an object
leaves the senses dry.

POSITIVE

I give you surfaces
of shiny fruit

hard slam of a door
enameled toilet seat

pretend porcelain
of the cheap cup

Georgia pine
teak of the islands

this glossy print
of three dimensions, taken

not made, at a glance.
How the man squints

and his lady blinks
away the sun

their flat features
buoyant as the boat

that holds
between wave and cloud.

I hand them over
to you. They're your
two parents, for sure.

Tap the surface of light.
See what happens

next, the negative event
instant in which

no picture was snapped:

the man's and the lady's
eyes clicked wide open.

I give you myself

only certain
of what's still

beneath the skin.
Take my arm

and I will bend
around you like a tree

and send up shoots
and follow light

until the end.

WHEN I WAS NOT DEAD

When I was not dead, no man
would marry me
for I would roam
in splotches of October,
need to notice my native
color: red, orange tending
yellow-brown,
sidelong glances
when contact tripped
me back, and I averted
my green eyes.

When I was not dead, urges
spurred my tramping.
Rustle, rustle, twig crunch.
Snappish, I flailed words,
hurled flat handshapes
to twirl midair, scatter
severed wings
at my laces looping debris.
And no man answered.
Where in this march my will
forced a season out of doors,
an equinox exchanging eyes
for leafy trails, for mounds
returning earthward,
I stumbled to disturb.

When I was not dead, the day
would claim its precedence
in hours of lost motion.
Muscles aching lessons,
I'd rest easy in
my bones, mind lent to leaves.
For twirls of foliage
I would snap the twig
of his snarled grip, release
the clinging strength
that follows need.

WHEN THIS YOU SEE

Viewfinder to eye,
lens cap stuck fast, I see
my reflected eye
turn back to blinking.

This shadow of water
casts light on the wall,
light basking in water,
a vertical sea. But seen through
a window, it's distance
clear as chance.

The days before this rain
were small but frequent
as smocked bodices
in that ticker tape of minutes:

the monster, remember,
she saw on this shore,
remember a wave washed the beast
with the head of a dog,
fins of a fish,
a body of thought she'd have missed
but for sight.

An exhibit of photographs,
black and white, by blind children:
so to be blind,
remember, is to see
nothing but motion. When anything moves
in front of the sun
they push the button
and the lone laughter shows. The shadows
they see, then, were always
in motion, this stage to that,
and the camera was seeing
what sight could not have,

what blind children might almost have
thought, and each thing ending
itself yet coded up with sense,
set out in shiftless language
in that laughter of the shutter click:
in that ticker tape of weeks, in that
ticker tape of months, in that
ticker tape of remember,
of years, years
of remember this, and this, and this.

PREVERBAL

A woman cups a fish of air before
she can open her eyes. I see
this woman you see bending down

before us, thirsty, feet scorched
by the hard walking surfaces
of this world. We intuit

danger in the manner that she waits;
hourly the handsome waves
lap her ankles, claim,

through the ritual intimacy of their
motions, to know her. But she, marooned
so long ago she has forgotten

name and age, must sit impassive.
Day after day, she remembers the way
it used to be, when in a city

of profusion, of lettuce and succulent
bamboo shoots, of watercress and fruits,
she still felt at times unsure

of basics, of gravity itself, as she
watched her fingers work avocado skin
away from the curved orbs,

her hands longing for this world,
even its cloudbursts, its boredom,
the spray of minutes that collects

while mushrooms are brushed clean,
as though all time and everything
could make her whole; as though a life,

in any amount, were sufficient to the task
of turning into love. And now she looks
to you, to me, thinking: *I would be*

leafy and green, were you to touch me
in preverbal morning, my tongue clinched
against reason, in recesses only teeth

admit, like a word that plums forth
and out, to erase my fear with daylight.
I remember the robin careened, its head

tilting from its body like a tired spring,
this sign I took to heart as I rinsed
my fingertips of stain. I am

holding here, to hear you tell me
that the wings of the robin, rising into
a glass sky, knew nothing of my wringing

doubt, died innocent, as only preverbal
lives can, never having burned
from irony, but never having trusted

death, confessed to song and its opposite.
I am waiting, half-blessed, to sip
the beads of water off your wrinkled palms.

WOMAN ONCE THOUGHT DEAD RECOVERING

*"I'm telling you, I've seen dead people 100 times in my
life, and she was dead. I saw a resurrection. I'm going
to my grave believing she had a second chance and this
is a miracle."*
     Champaign, Il. (AP)—Detective Gary Wright

I've been one of those
places they told you about
where frozen blossoms go
to meet blizzards and float
coloring the snow.
Cold melts the petals,
sun melts the snow.
Where I go
no one comes after.
The stretcher stung my skin
when I woke
seeing the blade float
over my throat. I swallowed.
The coroner dropped his knife,
and I rose, wrapped up
in this sack of flesh, a woman
back from death,
the coldest spring.
See, my fingertips
so pink, like petals of water,
until you touch them white
to know my story.

THIS DREAM OF MY CAT
AND MOTHER

Every woman paces her darkened house
trailing smoke, stalked by hungry meows
after a dream about
an internalized mother
and a favorite cat

whose perfect head—
just *there,* between the ears
(sleeping and waking),
bristling white hairs,
starbursts on black fur—bled

from a well-concealed wound,
and whose mouth, too,
produced rose pendants
the woman dabbed
but could not stanch

until her dream-mother appeared
and rubbed the grown
woman's back, as she had after long-

forgotten bad dreams
so a girl and every woman could fall asleep.

A LADY WRITING A
LETTER By VERMEER

All day I am walking to the square
in the sun. I don't know what to say.
I've begun the letter but it lies
on a black tile in the sitting room.
It has been five years
since the child. There's no reason
for delay. I sip tea, plead
with the bargain-maker, sass
the servant-girl, but no luck.
I take a pinch of chocolate, search
birds' tracks at the corners
of my eyes. No one knocks.
So what keeps me here?

It has taken this long to write.
Now, even you expect no reply.
That is as it should be.
I write to tell you I am alive.
What else is there? All the devils
you see in the air mean nothing—
this you know, so I write to assure you
you are not mistaken, your skin
is where you are not, around me
tight as stays. If I picture your face,
there is nothing left but this:
my stomach flowers as it once did.
I have not forgotten yet.

LADY READING A LETTER
AT THE OPEN WINDOW
By VERMEER

A woman faces the light
which nearly always falls
left to right in Vermeer.
Its source is clear
as the window, as the cloudless day.
She slants the page to sun, her face a mask
except for a tiny dagger of dark
beneath her eye. Her ghost
reflects full-face from panes of glass.
What's in the letter?

Half a peach tilted from
the Delft bowl bears its seed
upright on the bed. The remaining fruit
struggles to mound, large green apple
pushing red and orange and plum,
while a few soft pieces spill,
the half-cut peach is one. The painter's
favorite chair fills the corner—
its left lion shadow now.
In this example, we can see
that the chair is emptier
than the woman's hands
as she stands to read what the sun
tries to erase:

To you I send my only letter.
This is all you will hear from me.
Each morning as I've painted you from memory
we have grown apart.
You must not see this picture.
It is unjust. I have tried to paint us
in painting only you. The face
which pretends to be yours on the glass
is mine as you read this letter.

If you were able to adjust
the green curtain to your liking
you would discover my usual
Cupid, bow in one hand—
this letter raised in the other.

IN FOCUS

Last night I tumbled out
in failing light, a day before
the year's autumnal equinox,
to see by headlights, the way the road
unraveled past the tires' voice
and uneven heights of the outskirts'
built-up tangle. I headed south
by west, curved along the bypass
until the last exit that would shoot
me toward Pasolini's "Gospel
According to St. Matthew."

But in a stranded field, left
holding green between interstate
and convention hotels, malls and airport,
industrial parks, a cloud had found
a way to wedge between straw and the falling
dark, so that a thick, white field
of drifting energy lay ghostly flat
to match the field's dimensions
and to mask its bitter, mathematical scars.

It brought in focus the dead
and the living—a groundhog eyed traffic
from the shoulder—so that I checked
the rearview mirror to echo
what there was to be seen
just beyond, as if through a pinhole:
I swerved to give the animal room,
forgetting the anger that forced
me, like a paper narcissus,
into blooms of speed, forgetting
my failings, forgetting that I drove alone.
I traced my dry lips with a fingertip,
unwilling to kiss away the hurt
in a show of love. The field was real,
almost too real to see, until you might
follow my gaze with your eyes that know.

PRAYER UPON PARTING

Snakes in the grass abide
within the median green. Only
lawn Pedros, jockeys, fowl
and pale, peeling harts stare,
as we bend the careful corners of our
vernacular route, expectant of exotic
creatures all disappeared, extinct
as any dinosaur. But never mind,
forget them, Dear. I trust they've often
been just here, in this roiling field,
divided by telephone lines.

     If you can believe
in what you cannot see: if I can see
what you have given name, then
we can remember where we've been
though wander far and seldom speak.
It will be as when lovers must part
for wars in poetry.

          The women wait
for a return, ever cheerful in their toil.
Stars breathe and fizzle, even civilizations
build up by sticks and stones, wheel
on content, discontent, plus every other
in-between. While these women wait
inside their sturdy bamboo faith,
kept alive by the journey of another.

MY LIFE IN THE
SHELL OF AN EAR

Though it's a sore subject
much has been written
about the body
and how it loves.

This season snow pelts
lawn flamingos,
whorls of plastic, pink. But how
to tell you, you,
their wings are nothing, fake?

Last night when I talked
to your belly
        (you were asleep)
a curl I will refer
to here as truth
wound my ear
        (you were asleep)
a finger
echo within and without   and I
could hear
not you not me:

                    now
we are listening
through snowfalls
for what

PURITAN

Beyond the whitewash
of guilt
the sense that if you give
with one hand, hitting
away at the stone with the other
you have it beaten

No, I see through that rift
you're waiting simply
for a whitewash of guilt
to lift
you from your stained delay

Alone, you walk on stilts
a lilting in your tin-canned grace
you're looking for a way to sin
so silently no one will hear

The sips you tilt from glasses
won't intoxicate a lizard
you think it strange to stir
against the grain of plastic wood
when you would surely abdicate
if only, if you could

The vision pits you against your guilt
it's the last hour
and you must choose—it, or
a life you fear to lose your false
hope in—a stinging daily exercise:
you purify your guilt until it almost fits

All those in favor send you letters
you're their little starlet, you're so pitiful
and wise; fearing to criticize
they are your fans instead; they keep you
where you've been

But now the mountain accuses you
you thought you had the upper hand
but how it drums you down
it knows just where to hit the bone

Even your heart is not
what it might hone
Have you done enough for the homeless
have you become a home?

FEEDING THE FROZEN ANIMALS

All winter long
and it is a long winter
here, the frozen animals
attempt to thaw—
they crackle
like corn,
twitch like twigs,
buckle underfoot
like shoots of new grass.
The rangers buzz out,
airdrop bales of hay.
The frozen animals
circle. Food is suspect,
culprit, poison, and
too late in most cases,
but they must and do
chew even the ropes.
The frozen animals
climb down off the plateau,
climb down
from the hills, after leaving
the forest, frozen as slate,
they climb down,
and when they enter
the forest of lawn deer,
wander between swings
and boxwoods, lap the salt lick
of sand from the sandbox,
and bay, pressing their
noses to the kitchen
windowpane,
a woman at the sink faints
dead away.
Dear, it is only the frozen
animals—they come every year—
don't worry
they'll soon be dead.
He takes a sullen peach peel,
tosses it to the crusty snow,

pitches it at the hoofs
of the frozen animals
who have felt a bitter love
for green go haywire
in the snow.
Can there be so little light?
Can it be so?
Soon they stop altogether, soon they
stop together, shunning
contact with their hides.
Withered and ruffed
as husky fields,
they no longer recognize
their own kind
or scurry from people.
If they resemble themselves
after this, it is a miracle.
One dies for Science
on the windshield of a truck.
The biology class shudders
as the teacher carves;
they want to scrub
their hands with lye
after carefully cupping its heart.

FLIGHT LUCK

Apollo 13, can you hear us? This is Houston,
the future home of the Astros,
in the fisheye of mission control.
We are burning with reflections
on your three friends who were fired
in the multibillion-dollar kiln—one hell
of a spectacle. You see, this is Houston,
it was nonmetallic material that time,
in a pure environment
of oxygen, a tiny spark,
but we've fixed that now.
                              Galileo,
in 1610, invented a way to the moon;
he drew his own conclusions, sketched mare
in charcoal that still compares to photographs.
Sunspots incised twin stars
on the retinas of his eyes. The telescopic
limbs of light went out for him
one night.
               "Houston," we hear you calling,
"we've had a problem." But we thought
we had that solved, that's why we were dying
to defy the laws of luck, launch you charmed
at 1313 hours (someone's idea of a joke).
In just two days, it would occur
to us we might have made our second fatal
gaffe in much the same manner as our first.
This time, again, it was oxygen. A tank burst.
When we sent the ape, Ham, up, no one watched.
We never worried how to coach him down
to earth.
               Apollo crew, if you are orbiting,
reroute the poison gas, conserve water;
there are no lakes in space, alas. Eat light,
use your waste for ballast, and perhaps,
there's a chance, you will have enough
breath to see your flight back to us.
Good Luck.

LIGHTING THE DARK SIDE
OF THE MOON

"We'll see you on the other side," beamed Lovell
before he saw for the first time
the far side of the moon.
                              Christmas Eve,
sixty miles out—for thirty-four minutes
Apollo 8 occulted.
                         The lunar sphere, newsprint
adrift in a sea of stars, papier-mâché,
or a gray beach mound, felt
the scorch of jets.
Once the ship floated flawless in orbit,
TV sets tuned a blue Earthrise,
a mirage of living water on a slide:
we witnessed ourselves in the moon's eye.
Earth's turquoise islands sparked
cislunar distance; the astronauts listened
to the diamond stylus, to rhythmic seas inside
their dreams, as if shells crusted their ears
in curves of space.

Astronauts circled the stillborn moon;
like Arabian sheikhs, pitched their tent of night.
They logged the primeval homesickness,
slept fitful for our world of color.

FIVE YEARS FROM
THE LAST FIVE MINUTES
OF YOUR LIFE

So you've hedged your bets,
skinned your last easy cat
from the swingset's false horizon.

Now you're doomed to change,
accustomed to daylight, the fact
tadpoles sprout or drown trying.

Overnight, the time it takes
to muddle through your dreams
has left you high and half-

way on a path of
no return. So what
is it, is it that you want

to have, hold, to be-
come? Tell the inside out
of the wish you began with

before the real dream caked
your eyes with sleep, and waking
left you wistful. Tell

the dream you dreamed before
the words reshaped your longing
into a world your parents claimed.

It is five years, pretend, from
the last five minutes of your life;
where are you, with whom,

and what are you doing?
If you tell me you are
with a woman, I will ask her age,

ask the color of her scarf—
while you examine
and the cloth unfurls

a net two fishermen pull taut,
I will wait, rephrasing my next
question. What are the children's

names? *Hold on,* you interrupt,
I'm not so sure . . .
Tell me, I say, something you are

sure of. *Words wreck us,*
you answer, look out the window
where the dream trees have shed

their leaves, where the dream
cold rattles shingles into sense
and the dream of permanence

means death. There is always
sun to empty shadow,
slow transformation without comment.

ISLAND, PERHAPS

In days like these it rains after days of unease
before the rains would fall; the earth so dry,
that water falls away, runs off the back of the world
into basins and low country, country unlike this.
You wonder where the mountain got its name, and why
I persist in thinking of an island.
There's no surf here, no saltwater taffy
to pull us from our daily pains into a sleep that lulls
us into dreams. Like a remembered dream, the rain
falls, falling and racing in streams
along parched ground. It is barely summer, and you
stay far removed, in these mountains that I cling to,
while the world rains and I write this letter,
and you, perhaps, must push the thought of me
until it dislodges, spins, falls away to root
in someone else. You think of longing and my heart must
ache. I think of you and think that you must find it easy
not to remember me when the rain begins again.
That I cannot have the mountain and the ocean
is nothing in the scheme of things; that this rain
must be falling is nothing; that drought ends,
nothing; that I am remembering you
the way the earth finally remembers it has the power of rain
is like a catch in the throat, in time,
it will be nothing too.

A WAY TO DANCE

I wanted, then, to teach you how to love
But where my weight fell I could feel the snap
In time, the twig, rebroken, lost to prove.

Whatever I have told you was to move
Us beyond fear. No bodies were so rapt.
I wanted then to teach you how to love

The one I could become with new resolve:
Voice that will not shout; hand that will not slap.
In time, the twig, rebroken, just to prove

Its own redoubled worth, bent back and dove
Into the air. We could not help but clap.
I wanted then to teach you how to love

The way it fought the downdrafts, twirled to shove
Against mean gravity. Forget false maps.
In time, brave twig, rebroken, has to prove

Its way of dancing updrafts, Darling. Rove
Until your heart hits home, head on my lap.
I wanted, then, to teach you how to love.
This time, the twig, rebroken, has to prove.

THE FIREFLY GENE

Start with amorphous glitters of shadow
that rain the incline of red brick
when a flicker of flying   stars the corners of your vision.
At first you will think
you feel faint   because this
is something to believe in.   Start here
begin counting   the times
you have missed
                    mistrusting the simple drift of dreams.
From here I would nudge you   we might traverse
low along the ground   discover the grasses   the many names
for green   and from *forest*
                    if we begin rising
if we burst taller than Alice
our huge shadows darkening the land as sun lowers
touching danger to the whole long day apart.
If you would come with me
                    bow your gaze
before the light
fails us altogether   black and white cattle
fade to grey   our spectrum ebbs
while shoes clump into dark shapes and away   the pale
moon echoes what might have been.

There are no lessons to learn
the hard way here is *follow*
                    close your eyes
                              follow
Yet you stand in place hands folded   for merely blinking
holds its treachery   for most of our lives
we have felt this   since childhood   when the rattles
of night encircled
                    closing until we called out and out
and finally learned to keep to ourselves

when no one came   or someone came rubbing her eyes
to scold us back to sleep—
this was called growing up.
                              And now
I catch you up in opposites   ask you only
to awake   rise with me through incandescent
whirlwinds   to risk delirious pinwheels
ingest the firefly gene

TRAPEZIUMS

"Imagine a world alive with incomprehensible objects and shimmering with an endless variety of movement and innumerable gradations of color. Imagine a world before the 'beginning was the word.'"

—Stan Brakhage, *Metaphors on Vision*

Note no two sides ever parallel
but notice how even dust motes may glow
if just so the window floats
like a swiftly tilting liner
streaming tributaries of light
across the nexus of desire.
For how long have I been at sea?
For most of your life
the second person non sequitur to the self makes reply
its answer, comical yet serene,
in this specular plane of day upon day.

What would you have me say
for you? That I find loveliness in the shift
of waves into particles
in the back and forthness of the interchange itself?
That I go looking for waves, turn up particles,
content, go looking for particles in the ocean
of tick-tocking minutes; that I look
while I may still close my eyes and remember:

Gentle contours of clavicle,
the twist of wrist that opens your hand to touch
all the motions you would hide.
Or would you rather I lied?
Mention the motions I must go through until
I see you surfacing for air, until
stillness shakes us up to instruct
what movement really means.

Mention the weather, how it clouds us
into sense.
                    Today the sky
bounces blue cumulus
off a glass tabletop we sit down
to block with elbows, forks, and talk.
While inside and out the conversations
roll off tongues of metaphor,
of budding leaf and tulip stalk.
Earth sifting bottom to top
as I wander beneath the surface
spinning *table* into *desert,*
a fabulation meant to search
the cactus flower and the milk—

all the necessary conversions between us
and this earth
erase with our first words.

SEEING DISTANCE

*"Experience itself cannot be seen as a point in time, a
fact. . . . You read the poem: the poem you now have, the
poem that exists in your imagination, is the poem and
all the past to which you refer it."*
                              —Muriel Rukeyser, *The Life of Poetry*

The roots of desire
glance backward in time
as years removed by blinks
make light appearances,
scatter encoded paths
like finger taps.
These stars might
equal our missing mass,
eventually cause us to shrink.

But wait, this danger resurrects
a brambled, cobbled walk
where words cast faint quarks
between lifelines in a flutter
from long past.
Sticks in the throat,
pebbles and stones left
to stumble upon like crusted
patches of snow;
we must circumnavigate
to know how fingers thatch
the catch at the throat.
Through crackles and scratches
of an old gramophone
I think I hear what you're not
saying—yet—bouquets
of light/dark hair
retrace an afternoon pillow.

Where can we go but back
through cracks in the ice
before the star we see was born.
It is the past even now

as we close eyes, rummage
to compare but come up
dry. Our divining fails
the lost name in the glacier.
But we cannot stop this burning
imprint. Rub eyes and squint
against this ever-after wish.

Or the roots of an oak
taller than ancestral history
that seemed always
to hold its leaves.
I used to round this tree
in Grandmother's yard, trip
easily over its gnarled knees,
choking back tears,
vinegar-rinsed strands streaking
my hot forehead
not because of anything real.

      We skip into passages
      of time and out—our bodies
      barely here—so never fear
      the flicker—that's how
      we know—our bodies barely
      here—we can be healed.

At breakneck speed,
awaiting the going-home call
I'd twist in slick-soled Sunday best,
pearls tangled at my throat.
Careful, Grandmother would call
and wring her knotty hands,
Sweet child, watch your step now
while I would race—
the grown-ups talked—
race round, out of myself
forgetting where I was
but careful not to, not to fall.

THE TAUTOLOGY OF GOODBYE

You say I tend toward silences;
in these rifts, the world
I inhabit is a visual question,
marked by a balancing line
of light on distant water, a mirror
horizon. We afix binoculars
to what is real in this mirage:
a simple fishing rig, sunlight pouring
a swath of sea. I want your
hand to rest in mine, while I test
the real against the as yet
unknown, the present tense against
its picture: as the boat begins
to drift out of our range of vision,
we struggle to distinguish
the ruffles porpoises raise
from the action of waves.
It reminds me of the way our eyes
will try to meet in rearview
mirrors, of the loss I must suffer
whenever someone points
and I turn, but not in time.
I can feel the tugging
of the past in the way your fingers
almost pull away, then stay
to squeeze, and I know
just what it means
to grasp and then let go.

FOR MY COUSINS

Two bear cubs, little girls, I babysat
at the swimming pool. I remember how you liked to talk
more to each other than to me or to adults;
you understood your whispers, your worried expressions
when big boys you did not trust
splashed too close and I would assert my charge, pluck
you from their range; though I was closest to your age,
our common grandparents made me brave.
Riding home, I held the smallest of you in the backseat
and marveled between the shoestrings that tied your straps
at your downy back, brushed my fingers over
the light fur I had been teased about, at your age.
As I held you on my lap, still in your damp
stretch suit, the rocky fields and hayricks zoomed behind
the glass as I traced the length of your arm from fingertips
to shoulder, remembering the time I reached
down through water opaque with motion
to pick a sparkling quarter off the pool's rough finish
and my arm, so short, led my face into the depths.

Older versions of you, my sister and I would visit
your yard, walk its length to admire double-fist-sized
tomatoes coiling from dark soil, and hear
our father razz yours about his green thumb owing more
to the cemetery just over the fence,
than to Bonnie, our grandmother,
who gave both sons fine seeds from her prized German pink.

In the long dream of a winter night,
when Bonnie has been buried five springs or more,
buried on my birthday (it was your father
who remembered, after the graveside service, to order
my cake), I trace my feet, by flashlight,
over cold boards in a country house,
thinking milk might blur me back to sleep.
Before I can open the refrigerator door, the full moon
reveals the glowing backs of two pairs of black
cows, grazing as snow falls, oblivious, and I blink,
but the cows still eat. I think no more of milk

but marvel at white glaze on black grazing
through the night. Give us courage not to save
our best for bitter ends. Give us strength
to repeat what this earth wouldn't have us forget.

When we remember in winter we count up the dead.
True, it's no longer summer, and I'm no longer sure
whom I address
with these details from no more
than my life.
                    Winter finds me childless,
talking, perhaps, to the cousin who is left, perhaps
to her younger sister who has passed, about the way
memory fails to help us quite enough
to heal, about remembering when the fruit
and vine choked fence
could separate the living from the dead,
and every family
gathering was a mirror: two sons, their wives,
two daughters each in careful steps,
Bonnie Susan, Cathy; Catty, Bonnie Staley,
around the dark oak table.

But that was years ago, before we stopped
exchanging Christmas gifts, long before your granddaddy
died, or your mother, long before
the funeral when your friends came up to me,
speaking right into my face, "You look more
like her than the others."
"Yes. You remind me of your cousin."
And I thought then
of the week before, when I stood over you
and touched your frail back, all bone, to say goodbye,
yes, yes that's all we can do,
living and dying: remind us of each other.

for Catharine Hankla Clem, B. Susan Hankla, and in memory of
B. Staley Hankla, 1967–1988